**Angels descending,
bring from above,
echoes of mercy,
whispers of love.**

—FRANCES J. CROSBY,
"BLESSED ASSURANCE"

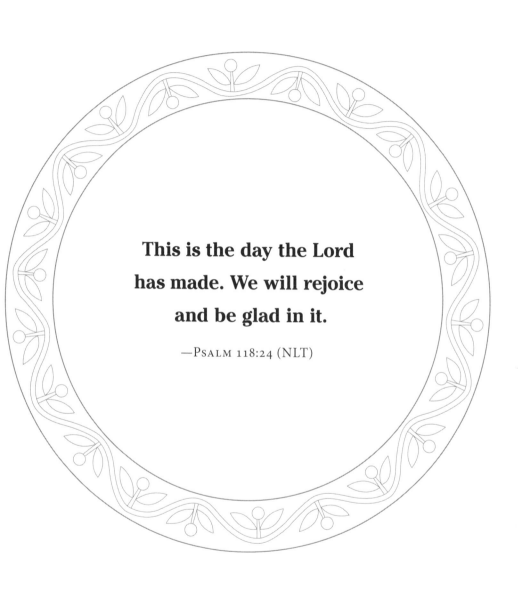

This is the day the Lord has made. We will rejoice and be glad in it.

—Psalm 118:24 (NLT)

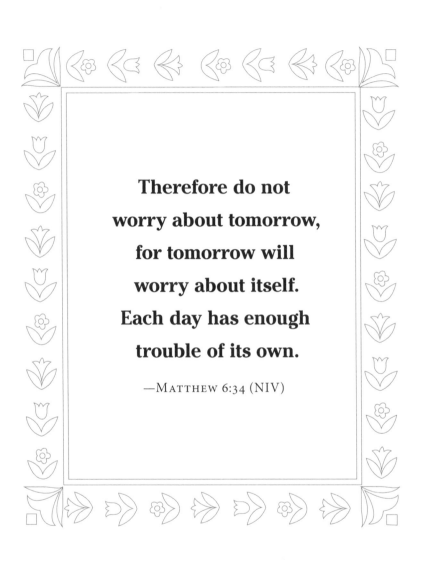

Therefore do not worry about tomorrow, for tomorrow will worry about itself. Each day has enough trouble of its own.

—Matthew 6:34 (NIV)

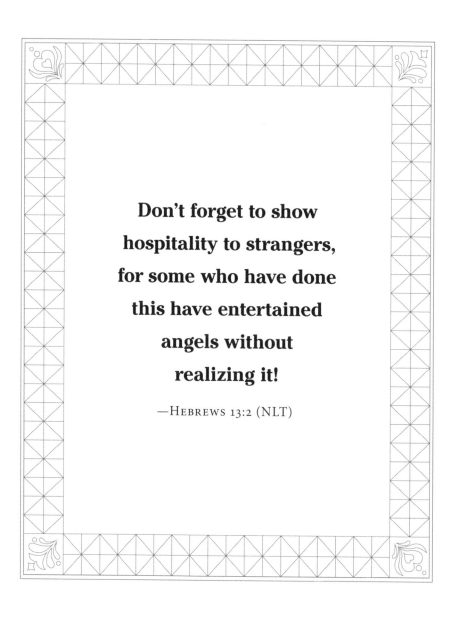

Don't forget to show
hospitality to strangers,
for some who have done
this have entertained
angels without
realizing it!

—HEBREWS 13:2 (NLT)

Believe in your infinite potential. Your only limitations are those you set upon yourself.

—ROY T. BENNETT,
THE LIGHT IN THE HEART

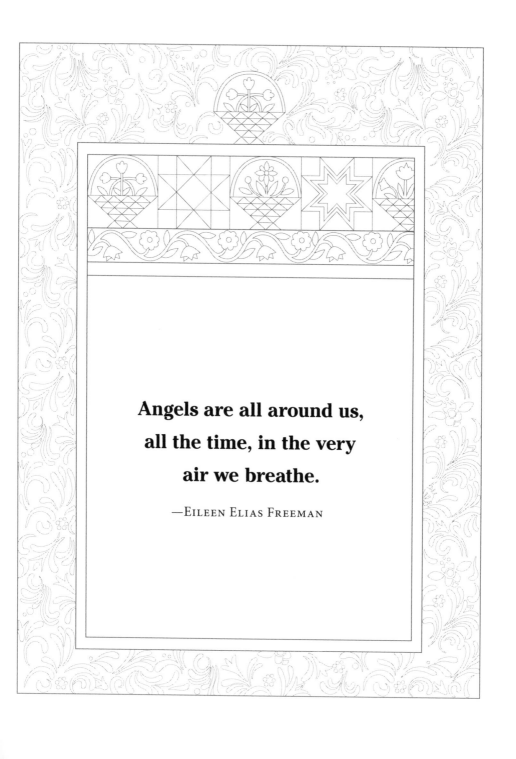

**Angels are all around us,
all the time, in the very
air we breathe.**

—Eileen Elias Freeman

Made in United States
Troutdale, OR
02/05/2024

17487969R10216

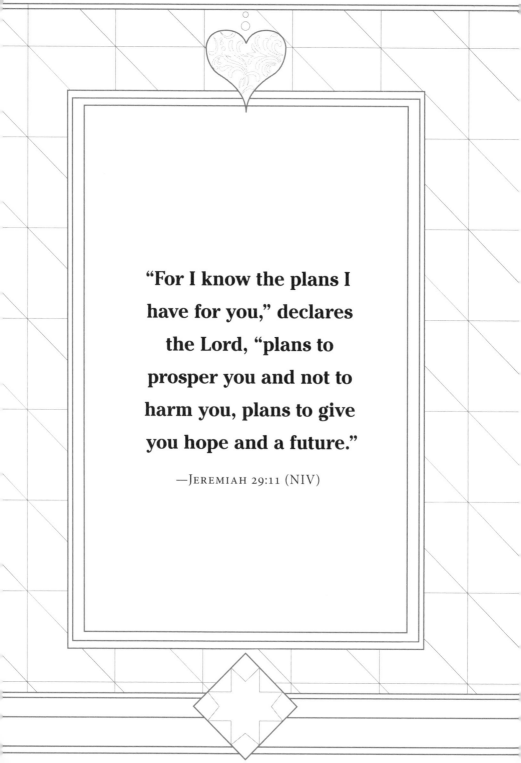

"For I know the plans I have for you," declares the Lord, "plans to prosper you and not to harm you, plans to give you hope and a future."

—JEREMIAH 29:11 (NIV)

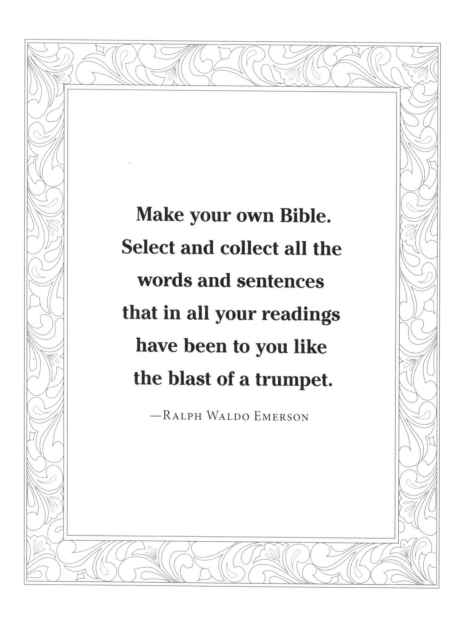

Make your own Bible.
Select and collect all the
words and sentences
that in all your readings
have been to you like
the blast of a trumpet.

—RALPH WALDO EMERSON

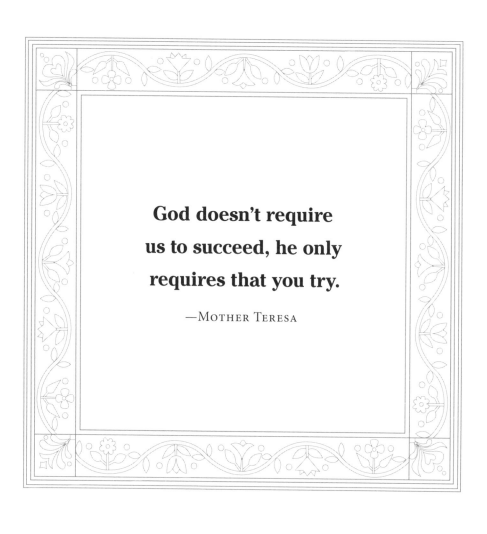

**God doesn't require
us to succeed, he only
requires that you try.**

—Mother Teresa

When angels visit us,
we do not hear the rustle
of wings, nor feel the
feathery touch of the
breast of a dove; but we
know their presence by
the love they create in
our hearts.

—MARY BAKER EDDY

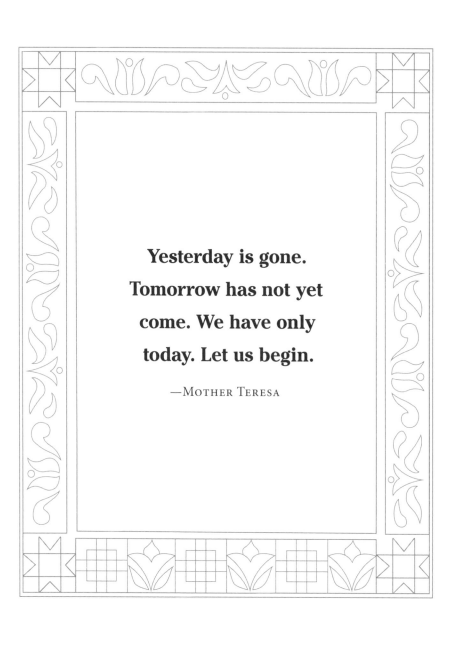

Yesterday is gone.
Tomorrow has not yet
come. We have only
today. Let us begin.

—Mother Teresa

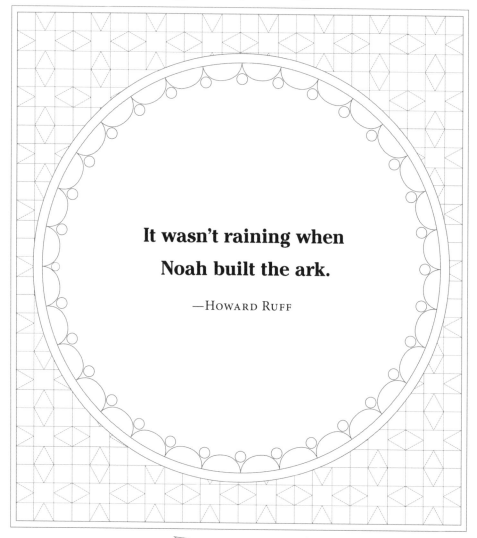

**It wasn't raining when
Noah built the ark.**

—Howard Ruff

About Jim Shore

Jim Shore grew up in rural South Carolina, the son of artistic parents who instilled a love of American folk art. His grandmother was a master quilter who taught him the patience and skill to bring intricate designs to life. Jim worked for decades developing his craft, manufacturing his own designs, and traveling the country to sell his work. Finally, in 2001, he partnered with Enesco to create Heartwood Creek, the successful brand that brought Jim worldwide fame. Jim has received multiple awards from prestigious trade organizations, including the ICON HONORS Life Accomplishment Award in 2012. Through his partnership with Enesco, the Jim Shore Collection has grown from a small group of Santas, snowmen, and angels to a broad year-round brand respected and sold around the world. Jim's boundless creativity and unique ability enable him to touch people in all walks of life through his art.

ISBN 978-1-64178-125-1

Fox Chapel Publishing makes every effort to use environmentally friendly paper for printing.

© 2021 by Jim Shore and Quiet Fox Designs, *www.QuietFoxDesigns.com*, an imprint of Fox Chapel Publishing Company, Inc., 903 Square Street, Mount Joy, PA 17552.

We are always looking for talented authors and artists. To submit an idea, please send a brief inquiry to acquisitions@foxchapelpublishing.com.

Printed in Singapore
First printing